5

LET'S
Student Book
GO

by
K. Frazier
B. Hoskins
R. Nakata

with
songs and chants by Carolyn Graham

Oxford University Press

Oxford University Press
198 Madison Avenue
New York, NY 10016 USA

Walton Street
Oxford OX2 6DP England

OXFORD is a trademark of Oxford University Press.

ISBN 0-19-434670-6

Editorial Manager: Shelagh Speers
Editors: June Schwartz, Sherri Arbogast, Paul Phillips
Project Manager: April Okano
Production Manager: Abram Hall

Cover design by April Okano
Cover Illustrations by Patrick Merrell and Paul Meisel

Continuing characters illustrated by Marcy Ramsey. Other interior
illustrations by David Coulson, Meryl Henderson, Lynn Jeffery,
Claudia Kehrhahn, Shelton Leong, Lauren Scheuer, Phil Scheuer
and Stacey Schuett.

Photo credits: Page 8 top to bottom David Barnes/Tony Stone Images,
L.L.T. Rhodes/Tony Stone Images and Ron Garrison/Zoological
Society of San Diego; Page 16 top Philip Dunn, bottom Ulrike Welsch;
page 33 left to right R. Kolar/Animals Animals, Renee Lynn/Photo
Researchers, Jerry Cooke/Photo Researchers, Chris Harvey/Tony
Stone Images, Robert Meier/Animals Animals, Tom McHugh/Photo
Researchers, Helen Cruickshank/Photo Researchers and Tim
Davis/Photo Researchers; page 44 top Randy Kalisek/F-Stock, bottom
Porterfield/Chickering/Photo Researchers; page 62 Michael
Newman/PhotoEdit; page 70 top to bottom French Government
Tourist Office, David Barnes/Tony Stone Images, Tony Craddock/Tony
Stone Images, H. Camille/French Government Tourist Office and
Explorer/Photo Researchers.

Production by Bill Smith Studio

Printing (last digit): 10 9 8 7 6 5 4 3 2 1

Printed in Hong Kong

Table of Contents

My name's Mark. I'm 12. I have one sister. She's 6. My best friend is Kevin. I like to play with my pets. I have two dogs and a bird. I also have some fish. I was a helper at the zoo during vacation.

Hi! I'm Beth. I'm 10 years old. I don't have any brothers or sisters. My best friend is Anna. I like to play computer games. I went to math camp during vacation.

I'm	Beth.	My	name's Mark.
	12.		best friend is Anna.
	10 years old.		

Ask and answer.

What's her name?
  Her name is Beth.

How old is she?
  She's 10 years old.

Does she have any brothers or sisters?
  No, she doesn't have any brothers or sisters.

What does she like to do?
  She likes to play computer games.

What did she do during vacation?
  She went to math camp.

1.

Beth
10
no brothers or sisters
play computer games
went to math camp

2.

Mark
12
one sister
play with his pets
was a helper at the zoo

3.

Anna
11
two brothers
play soccer
went to soccer camp

4.

Kevin
12
one brother and one sister
make models
visited his grandparents

What about you?

What's your name?
How old are you?
Do you have any brothers or sisters?

What do you like to do?
What did you do during vacation?
Who's your best friend?

Beth likes computers. Sometimes she writes stories on the computer, and sometimes she plays games. She wants to be a computer programmer.

Mark likes animals very much. He feeds his pets every day and gives them water. He wants to be a veterinarian.

Anna is a very good soccer player. Last Saturday she kicked a goal and won the game. She wants to be a coach.

Kevin likes to draw. He built a model rocket for the science fair and won first prize. He wants to be an engineer.

build → built

Ask the questions.

Here's an example.

A: What does she want to be?
B: She wants to be an engineer.

1.
A: _____?
B: She wants to be an engineer.

2.
A: _____?
B: She likes to play volleyball.

3.
A: _____?
B: He's going to play soccer

4.
A: _____?
B: She has to clean up her room.

5.
A: _____?
B: He wants to be a veterinarian.

6.
A: _____?
B: They're going to go shopping.

7.
A: _____?
B: He has to wash the dishes.

8.
A: _____?
B: They like to go camping.

Answer the questions.

1. What did they do yesterday?

2. What does he want to do?

3. Why did she stay home yesterday?

4. Which one is bigger?

Karlie's Report

Animals in zoos live in many different kinds of homes. Usually animals live in cages or behind fences. You can watch these animals, but you can't feed or pet them.

In a petting zoo, small or gentle animals live in barns or inside pens. You can touch and feed the animals, and sometimes you can go inside the pens with them.

In a wild animal park, the animals are free. They don't live in cages or behind fences. Their homes in the zoo look like their homes in the wild. You have to stay inside a bus or train and ride through the zoo to see them.

During vacation, I went to the San Diego Zoo. I saw all of these animal homes.

New Words

different	gentle
kinds of	barns
cages	pens
fences	wild animal park
pet	look like
petting zoo	wild

Answer the questions.

1. Where do zoo animals usually live?
2. What can you do in a petting zoo?
3. Can you touch the animals in a wild animal park?
4. Where did Karlie go during vacation?

True or false?

1. Zoo animals always live in cages.
2. You can't touch the animals in a petting zoo.
3. In wild animal parks, the animals are free.
4. You have to stay inside a bus or train in a wild animal park.

Choose a title.

Which is the best title for Karlie's report?

a. All About Animals
b. Animal Homes in Zoos
c. A Ride Through the Zoo

Vocabulary

What does "pet" mean?

a. touch
b. watch
c. feed

What about you?

Do you ever go to the zoo?
What kinds of animals do you like to see?
What kinds of homes do they live in?

Sounds and Sentences

snail

snack

snow

The snail likes to eat a snack in the snow.

small

smear

smile

The small boy smeared the paint and smiled.

She Wants to Be an Engineer

She wants to be an engineer.
She wants to be an engineer.
Her mother was an engineer,
Her father was one, too.
She wants to be an engineer.

She doesn't want to be a nurse.
She doesn't want to be a sailor.
She doesn't want to be an English teacher.
She wants to be an engineer.

She wants to be an engineer.
She doesn't want to be a lawyer.
She doesn't want to be a rich man's wife,
Oh, no. She wants to be an engineer,
Just like her mama.
She wants to be an engineer.

Listen and number the boxes.

Listen and circle.

Listen to the answer and check the question.

1. ☐ What did she do yesterday?
   ☐ What is she going to do?

2. ☐ What does he like to do?
   ☐ What does he have to do?

3. ☐ What does she want to be?
   ☐ What does she do?

4. ☐ Who's his best friend?
   ☐ Who's his brother?

Anna: Hi, Mark!
Mark: Hi, Anna. Are you going somewhere?
Anna: Yes, I'm going to visit my cousins. What about you?
Mark: I'm not going anywhere. I'm waiting for my aunt.

Anna: What does she look like?
Mark: She's tall and she has short hair.
Anna: Is that her over there?
Mark: No, that's not her. My aunt has blond hair and she wears glasses.
Anna: Is that her next to the bench?
Mark: Yes, it is. Thanks, Anna.

Mark: Aunt Mary, here I am!

Anna: Well, I have to go now. My train is leaving in five minutes.
Mark: OK. Have a good trip.
Anna: Thanks. See you Monday.

Have a good trip.
   Thanks. See you Monday.

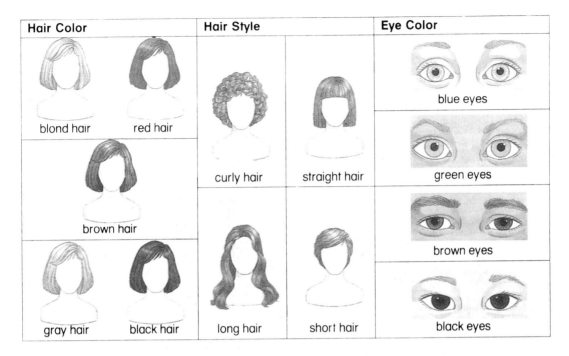

Hair Color	Hair Style	Eye Color
blond hair red hair	curly hair straight hair	blue eyes
brown hair		green eyes
gray hair black hair	long hair short hair	brown eyes
		black eyes

Ask and answer.

What does he look like?
     He has red hair and green eyes.

1.	2.	3.	4.
5.	6.	7.	8.

Anna's train is coming into the station. Her aunt, uncle, and cousins are waiting for her. Her aunt is the woman in the blue and yellow dress. Her uncle is the man with glasses and red hair. Her cousin Maria is the girl with long brown hair. Her cousin Pedro is the boy in the yellow cap.

Grammar Focus	
Her uncle is the man	with red hair.
Her aunt is the woman	in the yellow cap.
Her cousin is the girl	
Her cousin is the boy	

Ask and answer.

Which girl is Brian's cousin?
His cousin is the girl | with curly red hair.
| in the blue pants and striped shirt.

BRIAN'S FAMILY

| 1. cousin | 2. aunt | 3. grandfather | 4. older brother | 5. mother |
| 6. younger brother | 7. father | 8. sister | 9. grandmother | 10. uncle |

Play a game.

Ask questions about the pictures above. Here's an example.

A: I'm thinking of a man.
B: Is he the man with blond hair?
A: No, he isn't.
B: Is he the man with gray hair?

A: Yes, he is.
B: Is he Brian's grandfather?
A: Yes, he is.

Allison's Report

This is a report about two families. One family is a small family and the other family is a big one.

This is Diane. She is my cousin. She lives in England. She has a small family. She lives with her father, mother, and sister. They live in an apartment. Diane's grandparents live far away. Diane and her family visit them once a year.

This is Roberto. He is my pen pal. He lives in Chile. He has a big family. He lives with his father, mother, brothers, sisters, and grandparents. They live in a big house. His aunt and uncle and cousins live in a house next door. They see each other every day.

New Words

other	once a year
England	Chile
apartment	next door
far away	each other

Answer the questions.

1. Does Diane have a big family or a small family?
2. Why doesn't she see her grandparents every day?
3. Where does Roberto live?
4. How often does Roberto see his cousins?

True or false?

1. Diane lives far away from her grandparents.
2. Roberto has a small family.
3. Roberto's cousins live far away.
4. Diane visits her grandparents every year.

Choose a title.

Which is the best title for Allison's report?
a. Two Kinds of Families
b. Diane's Family
c. Roberto's Family

Vocabulary

What does "grandparents" mean?
a. mother and father
b. aunt and uncle
c. grandmother and grandfather

What about you?

Do you have a big family or a small family?
How many people live with you?
How often do you see your grandparents?

Sounds and Sentences

swallows

swan

swing

swoop

The swallows swooped down near the swan on the swing.

twinkling

twins

twirl

twilight

The twins twirled in the twinkling twilight.

Who's That Girl?

Who's that?
Who's that?
Who's that girl? Who's that?
Who's that girl in the short black dress?
    That's my older sister, Bess.

Who's that?
Who's that?
Who's that boy? Who's that?
Who's that boy with the baseball bat?
    That's my younger brother, Pat.

Who's that woman in the long red skirt?
Who's that man in the bright green shirt?
Who's that boy with the curly hair?
Who's that girl with the teddy bear?

    That's my mother in the long red skirt.
    That's my father in the bright green shirt.
    That's my brother with the curly hair.
    That's my sister with the teddy bear.

Listen and circle

Listen and number the pictures.

A. Fill in the blanks. Then say and act.

1. **Beth:** What's his name?
   Mark: _____ Tom.
   Beth: _____?
   Mark: Yes, he has one sister.

2. **Anna:** _____?
   Mark: She's tall and she has short hair.
   Anna: Is that her over there?
   Mark: No, _____.
   My aunt has blond hair and she wears glasses.

B. Ask your partner.

What did you do yesterday?
What are you going to do tomorrow?
What do you like to do?
What do you have to do after school?

C. Answer the questions.

What do you look like?
What does your teacher look like?
What does your best friend look like?

D. Listen to the answers. Number the questions.

_____ What does he look like?
_____ Where did she go during vacation?
_____ What does she like to do?
_____ What is she doing?
_____ What is he going to do after school?

E. Listen and number the pictures.

☐   ☐   ☐   ☐   ☐

Beth: Hi, Anna! What are you doing?
Anna: I'm packing the car. We're going to go camping.
Beth: That sounds like fun!

Anna's mother: What are you going to do this weekend, Beth?
Beth: I don't know. Nothing much.
Anna's mother: Would you like to go camping with us?
Beth: Sure! I'd love to. But first I have to ask my parents.

Anna: Hello?
Beth: Hi, Anna. This is Beth. Good news! i can go camping with you.
Anna: Great!
Beth: What will I need?
Anna: You'll need a sleeping bag and a pillow. Bring some warm clothes, too. It'll be cold at night.
Beth: OK. I'll be at your house in twenty minutes.
Anna: Good. See you soon!

Would you like to go camping with us?
    Sure! I'd love to.
    Thanks, but I can't.

I would = I'd

Ask and answer.

He's going to go camping **tomorrow**.
What will he need?
   He'll **need** a tent **and** a flashlight.

I will = I'll
You will = You'll
He will = He'll

She will = She'll
It will = It'll
They will = They'll

1. go camping

2. play baseball

3. play tennis

4. go swimming

a towel
a tennis ball
a baseball bat
a bathing suit
a tent
a flashlight
a tennis racquet
TENT

Say these.

It'll be cold tomorrow.
I'll need a jacket.

It'll be hot tomorrow.
I won't need a jacket.

HOT
WARM
COOL
COLD

will not = won't

Anna, her family, and Beth are on their way to the campground. Anna and Beth are planning their camping trip.

Tomorrow morning they'll go hiking. In the afternoon they'll go canoeing.

On Sunday morning they'll go fishing and then they'll go swimming.

Every night they'll have a campfire. It'll be fun!

Ask and answer.

What will they do tomorrow?
    They'll go canoeing.

1. go canoeing

2. have a picnic

3. go fishing

4. go hiking

5. have a campfire

6. go bird watching

Yes or no?

Ask questions about the pictures above.

Will they need a canoe?   Yes, they will.
                           No, they won't.

a canoe

a paddle

a life jacket

a thermos

hiking boots

binoculars

a fishing pole

bait

a backpack

a picnic basket

Steve's Report

Leaves have many different shapes. You can make beautiful pictures with leaves and paint. Here's a fun project.

First, find some leaves. Then get some paper, paint, paintbrushes, and glue. Glue the leaves onto the paper. Don't use too much glue. Wait for an hour. Then paint over the leaves and the paper. Let the paint dry overnight. In the morning, carefully peel the leaves off the paper. You will see a beautiful leaf pattern.

There are many things you can make with your leaf pictures. You can make birthday cards or wrapping paper.

New Words

shapes	hour
project	overnight
paintbrushes	peel off
onto	pattern
too much	birthday cards
wait	wrapping paper

Answer the questions.

1. Do all leaves have the same shape?
2. What do you need to make leaf pictures?
3. How long do you let the paint dry?
4. What can you make with leaf pictures?

Put the steps in order.

_____ Paint over the leaves.
_____ Peel the leaves off the paper.
_____ Glue the leaves onto some paper.
_____ Find some leaves.

Choose a title.

Which is the best title for Steve's report?
a. Making a Birthday Card
b. Collecting Leaves
c. Leaf Pictures

Vocabulary

What does "overnight" mean?
a. two hours
b. all day
c. through the night

What about you?

Do you like to collect leaves?
What else can you do with leaves?

Sounds and Sentences

skeleton

skirt

skate

skunk

The skeleton in the skirt is skating around the skunk.

schedule

scholars

school

The scholars looked at the school schedule.

Unit 3

The Weatherman Song

Weatherman, weatherman, listen to me.
How will the weather be?
How will the weather be?
Weatherman, weatherman, listen to me.
How will the weather be tomorrow?

Will it rain?
    No, no.
Will it snow?
    No, no.
Will the sun come out?
    I don't know. I don't know.
Will the stars be bright in the sky tonight?
Will it be all right?
    I don't know.

Weatherman, answer me, yes or no?
Will it rain tomorrow? Will it snow?
Answer me, weatherman, yes or no?
Will it rain tomorrow? Will it snow?

Will it rain?
    No, no.
Will it snow?
    No, no.
Will the moon come out?
    I don't know. I don't know.
Will the stars be bright in the sky tonight?
Will it be all right?
    I don't know.

Listen and check.

1.
☐ Yes, he will.
☐ No, he won't.

2.
☐ Yes, she will.
☐ No, she won't.

3.
☐ Yes, they will.
☐ No, they won't.

4.
☐ Yes, he will.
☐ No, he won't.

5.
☐ Yes, she will.
☐ No, she won't.

6.
☐ Yes, they will.
☐ No, they won't.

Listen and check.

	🎣	🎾	🧤	⚾	⚾	🏝	BAIT	🏏
Miku								
Mario								
Lindsay								
Kent								

Mark: I'm worried about the math test tomorrow. Math is so hard.
Beth: No, it isn't. It's easy.
Mark: Not for me. I don't like numbers. Geography is easy, but not math.

Beth: I think geography is harder than math.
Mark: No, it isn't. Geography is easier. It's about real places. It's more fun!
Beth: Not for me. I don't like maps.

Mark: Hey, Kevin. What do you think?
Kevin: Well, I think geography is easy.
Mark: I think so, too.
Kevin: But math is easy, too. They're both easy for me!

What do you think?
  I think geography is easy.

easy → easier
hard → harder

Say these.

I think geography is **easy.**
I think geography is **easier than** math.

I think math is **hard.**
I think math is **harder than** geography

Play a game.
Toss two coins onto the game board. Make a sentence.

I think English is	harder easier	than art.

English

art

math

science

history

geography

literature

music

physical education

Ask your partner.
Which subject is easier, _____ or _____?
Which subject is harder, _____ or _____?
What's your favorite subject?

Mark has to make a report about animals for his science class. He went to the library and asked the librarian for help. She showed him some good books about animals.

Mark read about the speeds and sizes of many different animals. He took a lot of notes.

He compared the speeds of several animals. He was surprised. The jackrabbit is **as fast as** the racehorse and it is **faster than** the greyhound. The cheetah is **the fastest** animal on land.

At home, Mark looked at his notes again. Then he made a chart for his report.

Grammar Focus

---

fast → faster → the fastest

Ask and answer. Compare the animals.

greyhound
64 kph

fox
64 kph

racehorse
72 kph

cheetah
110 kph

cat
48 kph

kangaroo
64 kph

jackrabbit
72 kph

gazelle
80 kph

1. Which one is the fastest?   The _____ is the fastest.
2. Which one is the slowest?   The __ _____ is the slowest.
3. Which one is the biggest?   The _____ is the biggest.
4. Which one is the smallest? The _____ is the smallest.

Make sentences about the chart above.

1. Use *bigger, smaller, slower,* and *faster.*
   The racehorse is bigger than the jackrabbit.
2. Use *as fast as.*
   The fox is as fast as the kangaroo.

Unit 4

Rick's Report

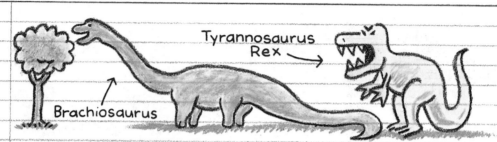

Dinosaurs lived millions of years ago. Some dinosaurs were very big and some were very small. Some walked and some flew.

The biggest dinosaur was the Brachiosaurus. It was taller than all the other dinosaurs. The Brachiosaurus ate leaves and plants.

The smallest dinosaur was the Compsognathus. It was smaller than a chicken. It had feathers, too. The Compsognathus ate small animals.

The meanest dinosaur was the Tyrannosaurus Rex. The other dinosaurs were afraid of it because it was very fierce and it liked to fight. It had sharp teeth and ate smaller dinosaurs and other animals.

There are no dinosaurs today, but you can see dinosaur bones in a natural history museum.

New Words

dinosaur	Tyrannosaurus Rex
millions of years ago	afraid
Brachiosaurus	fierce
plants	fight
Compsognathus	sharp
feathers	bones
mean	natural history museum

Answer the questions.

1. When did dinosaurs live?
2. Did any dinosaurs fly?
3. What did the Tyrannosaurus Rex eat?
4. Which dinosaur was the biggest?

True or false?

1. The Brachiosaurus was the meanest dinosaur.
2. The Compsognathus was smaller than a chicken.
3. Today dinosaurs live in zoos.
4. You can see dinosaur bones in a natural history museum.

Choose a title.

Which is the best title for Rick's report?
a. Dinosaurs
b. The Brachiosaurus and the Compsognathus
c. Natural History Museums

Vocabulary

What does "fierce" mean?
a. likes to eat
b. likes to fly
c. likes to fight

What about you?

Which dinosaur do you like the best? Why?

Sounds and Sentences

stork

stagecoach

storm

The stagecoach was faster than the stork in the storm.

strawberries

stroller

stream

Andy ate strawberries in a stroller by the stream.

An Elephant is Bigger Than a Flea

An elephant is bigger than a flea.
I said an elephant is bigger than a flea.
An elephant is stronger.
An elephant lives longer.
An elephant is bigger than a flea.

An elephant is better than a flea.
    Why?
Because an elephant is easier to see in the dark.
An elephant is bigger, much, much bigger.
An elephant is bigger than a flea.

A crocodile is bigger than a fly.
I said a crocodile is bigger than a fly.
A crocodile is stronger.
A crocodile lives longer.
A crocodile is bigger than a fly.

A crocodile is better than a fly.
    Why?
Because a crocodile can smile and he can cry.
A crocodile is better.
He can even knit a sweater.
A crocodile is better than a fly.

Listen and check the answer.

1. [ ] He thinks science is harder than literature.
   [ ] He thinks science is easier than literature.

2. [ ] She thinks history is harder than music.
   [ ] She thinks history is easier than music.

3. [ ] He thinks math is harder than geography.
   [ ] He thinks geography is harder than math.

4. [ ] She thinks English is easier than art.
   [ ] She thinks art is easier than English.

Listen. Which words do you hear? Circle the words.

1. history
   geography
   music
   English

2. art
   literature
   science
   math

3. physical education
   English
   music
   art

4. math
   science
   history
   literature

Listen and circle the word.

1.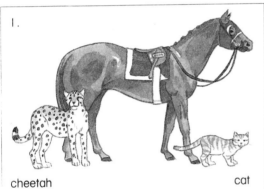

cheetah   cat

2.

kangaroo   fox   gazelle

3.

jackrabbit   fox   cheetah
72 kph   64 kph   110 kph

4.

jackrabbit   greyhound   cat
72 kph   64 kph   48 kph

Let's Review

A. Fill in the blanks. Then say and act.

1. **Anna's mother:** What are you _____ this weekend, Beth?
   Beth: I don't _____. Nothing much.
   Anna's mother: _____ go camping with us?
   Beth: Sure, _____.

2. **Mark:** _____ easier, geography or math?
   Beth: Well, I think _____.
   Mark: Hey Kevin, _____think?
   Kevin: I think _____, but _____, too. They're both easy for me.

B. Ask your partner. Circle the answer.

What do you think? Is English easy or hard?

English	easy	hard	literature	easy	hard
math	easy	hard	history	easy	hard
geography	easy	hard	music	easy	hard
art	easy	hard	science	easy	hard

C. Answer the question.

What are you going to do this weekend?

D. Listen to the questions. Circle the answers.

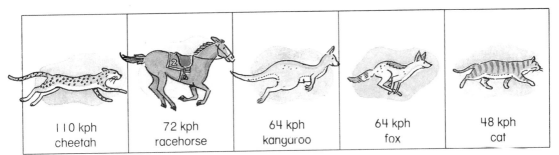

110 kph cheetah	72 kph racehorse	64 kph kangaroo	64 kph fox	48 kph cat

1. cheetah
   racehorse
   cat
   fox

2. racehorse
   fox
   cat
   kangaroo

3. fox
   kangaroo
   cheetah
   racehorse

4. kangaroo
   cheetah
   racehorse
   fox

E. Play a game. Ask and answer.

A: I'm going to go camping.
B: What will you need?
A: I'll need _____.

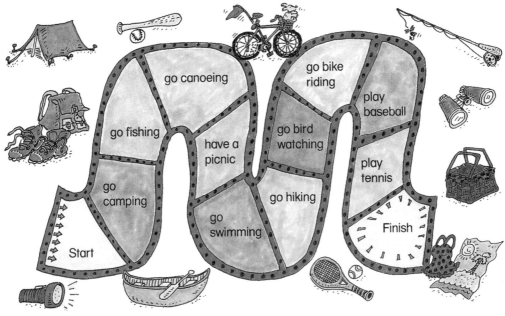

Beth: I hate winter. I'm tired of the cold and snow.
Anna: Not me! Winter is my favorite season.
Beth: Why?
Anna: Because I like skiing.

Anna: Which season do you like best?
Beth: I like summer best because I like swimming.
Anna: Oh, look! There's Mark. Let's catch up with him.
Beth: OK.

Anna: Hey, Mark. Wait for us.
Mark: OK, but please hurry up. I'm cold.
Anna: We're walking as fast as we can.

Beth: Oh, no! Not again!

Wait for	us.
	me.
OK.	

Seasons

winter   spring   summer   fall

Ask and answer.

Why does he like winter best?
He likes winter best because he likes ice skating.

1. ice skating
2. water skiing
3. planting flowers
4. jumping into leaves
5. swimming
6. playing football
7. skiing
8. flying kites

What about you?

Which season do you like best? Why?

Last summer Kevin and his family went to a dude ranch. They made a lot of new friends.

Every day Kevin worked outside with the ranch hands and rode a horse.

At night everyone ate dinner around a campfire. Then the ranch hands told stories.

Kevin and his family had a really good time. Next summer they're going to go back there again.

Grammar Focus		
past	**now**	**future**
yesterday	today	tomorrow
last week	this week	next week
last month	this month	next month
last year	this year	next year

Ask and answer.

What did she **do** last summer?
   She **went** to a dude ranch.
What's she **going to do** next summer?
   She's **going to go** to the beach.

1.
last summer   next summer

2.
yesterday   tomorrow

3.
last month   next month

4.
last week   next week

What about you?

What grade were you in last year?
What grade will you be in next year?

Vincent's Report

I always thought December was the coldest month of the year. But last year I learned something new about seasons. Different parts of the world have winter, spring, summer, and fall at different times of the year.

I live in Minnesota in the United States. In December it's winter here. It's cold and there is a lot of snow and ice. During winter vacation I usually go skiing and ice skating.

December in Minnesota

Last year I went to Australia during winter vacation. I was surprised. In December it was summer there. The weather was hot and sunny. I went swimming and sailing every day.

December in Australia

The seasons are different in the United States and Australia because they are at opposite sides of the world. When it's spring in the United States, it's fall in Australia. When it's summer in the United States, it's winter in Australia.

New Words

thought
something
parts of the world
times of the year
Minnesota

the United States
ice
Australia
sailing
opposite sides

Answer the questions.

1. Is it hot and sunny in Minnesota in December?
2. What does Vincent usually do during winter vacation?
3. Where is it summer in December?
4. Why are the seasons different in the United States and Australia?

True or false?

1. All parts of the world have winter, spring, summer, and fall at the same time of the year.
2. There is a lot of snow and ice in Minnesota in December.
3. You can go swimming and sailing in December in Australia.
4. When it's spring in the United States, it's summer in Australia.

Choose a title.

Which is the best title for Vincent's report?
a. Skiing
b. Sailing
c. Seasons

Vocabulary

What does "seasons" mean?
a. winter, spring, summer, fall
b. January, February, March
c. Monday, Tuesday, Wednesday

What about you?

In your country, which months are winter?
Which months are summer?
What can you do in your country in the winter?

Sounds and Sentences

squid

squeezed

square

The squid squeezed into the little square.

queen

question

quiz

The queen answered the question on the quiz.

Last Summer, What Did You Do?

Last summer, what did you do?
   I went to Hawaii.
I did, too.
Did you buy anything?
   Yes, I did. I bought a two-dollar tie.
So did I.

Last winter, where did you go?
   I went to London.
So did Joe.
Did you buy anything?
   Yes, I did. I bought English tea.
So did he.

Next winter, what are you going to do?
   We're going to go skiing.
We are, too.
Next summer, where are you going to be?
   We're going to stay home.
So are we.

Listen and check.

1. Winter is Norman's favorite season.
   Spring is Norman's favorite season.

2. Summer is Brenda's favorite season.
   Fall is Brenda's favorite season.

3. Winter is Brian's favorite season.
   Summer is Brian's favorite season.

4. Jessica and Donna like fall best.
   Jessica and Donna like spring best.

5. Pete and Jason like fall best.
   Pete and Jason like winter best.

6. Allison likes winter best.
   Allison likes summer best.

Listen to the answers and check the questions.

1. What did she do yesterday?

   What is she going to do tomorrow?

2. What did he do last month?

   What is he going to do next month?

3. What are they going to do next week?

   What did they do last week?

4. What is he going to do next summer?

   What did he do last summer?

5. What did she do last week?

   What is she going to do next week?

6. What are they going to do tomorrow?

   What did they do yesterday?

Kevin: I'm hungry! Why don't we make a snack?

Mark: That's a good idea. I'm hungry, too. What do you have to eat?

Kevin: Well, there's some peanut butter and jelly and some bread in the cupboard. And there are some potato chips and some bananas, too.

Mark: Great!

Kevin: Is there anything in the refrigerator?

Mark: Let's see. There's some ham and cheese, and there are some pickles.

Kevin: Perfect! Let's use it all.

Why don't we make a snack?
That's a good idea.
No, I don't want to.

Say these.

There **is** some juice.
There **is** some cake.

There **are** some cookies.
There **are** some knives.

Ask and answer.

What's in the blue picnic basket?
   There is some cake and there are some plates.

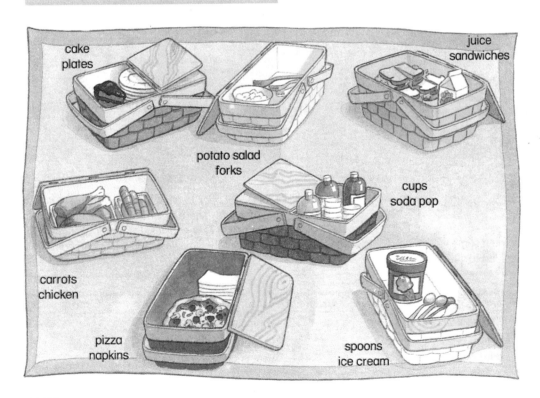

cake
plates

juice
sandwiches

potato salad
forks

cups
soda pop

carrots
chicken

pizza
napkins

spoons
ice cream

Last week Beth and her family went to a picnic Beth was very hungry. She put **a lot of** food on her plate.

Then she saw the desserts. There were **a lot of** cookies and there was a big chocolate cake. Everything looked delicious.

Beth wanted some cake, but her plate was full. She decided to get dessert later.

Beth went back to get some dessert, but she was too late. There was no cake and there were only **a few** cookies. Beth was very disappointed. Next time, she's going to eat dessert first!

Grammar Focus

How much cake is there?

There is **a little** cake.
There is **a lot of** cake.

How many cookies are there?

There are **a lot of** cookies.
There are **a few** cookies.

Ask and answer.

How much water is there?		
There is	a little	water.
	a lot of	

How many oranges are there?		
There are	a few	oranges.
	a lot of	

1. water

2. orange juice

3. lemonade

4. milk

5. oranges

6. apples

7. bananas

8. peaches

Make sentences.

There is	a little	_____ .
	a lot of	

There are	a few	_____ .
	a lot of	

Rachel's Report.

Food scientists made this pyramid to help you choose healthy food. You need to eat a lot of the food at the bottom of the pyramid and only a little of the food at the top.

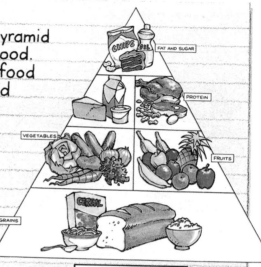

FOOD PYRAMID

You need to eat a lot of grains, like rice and bread, every day. You also need to eat a lot of vegetables, like carrots and spinach. Fruits, like apples and oranges, are very important, too.

Every day you need to eat some protein. It helps you grow. There is protein in milk, cheese, fish, and eggs.

The food at the top of the pyramid has a lot of fat or sugar. This food is in the smallest part of the pyramid because you don't need much fat or sugar.

Try to use the food pyramid every day and you will stay healthy.

New Words

pyramid	fruits
healthy	important
bottom	protein
top	grow
grains	fat
vegetables	sugar
spinach	try

Answer the questions.

1. Why did food scientists make the food pyramid?
2. Which food is a vegetable, a carrot or an orange?
3. Is there protein in cheese?
4. Why are sugar and fat in the smallest part of the pyramid?

True or false?

1. You need to eat a lot of sugar and fat every day.
2. There is protein in fish.
3. Apples are vegetables.
4. You need to eat a lot of the food at the bottom of the pyramid.

Choose a title.

Which is the best title for Rachel's report?
a. Food
b. Fruits and Vegetables
c. The Food Pyramid

Vocabulary

What does "healthy" mean?
a. not hungry
b. not sick
c. not happy

What about you?

What did you eat for dinner last night? Which groups on the food pyramid did your dinner come from?

Sounds and Sentences

spring

sprouts

spruce

I see sprouts on the spruce in the spring.

splish

splash

splatter

Splish, splash, splatter! Down went the platter!

How Much Do You Want?

How much do you want?
    Not too much.
    Just a little.
    Not too much.

    A little of this
    And a little of that.
    Just a little.
    Not too much.

How many do you want?
    Not too many.
    Just a few.
    One or two.

    A few of these
    And a few of those.
    Just a few.
    One or two.

Not too much.
Just a little.
Not too many.
Just a few.

    Not too much.
    Just a little.
    Just a few.
    One or two.

Listen and check.

1. Brett				
2. Kathy				
3. Eric				
4. June				

True or false? Listen and circle the answer.

1. true
   false

2. true
   false

3. true
   false

4. true
   false

5. true
   false

6. true
   false

7. true
   false

8. true
   false

A. Fill in the blanks. Then say and act.

1. **Anna:** Winter is my favorite season.
   Beth: _____?
   Anna: Because _____.
   Which season _____?
   Beth: I like summer best because
   _____.

2. **Kevin:** I'm hungry. Why don't we _____?
   Mark: That's a good idea. I'm _____, too.
   What _____?
   Kevin: Well, there's some _____
   in the cupboard. And there are some
   _____, too.
   Mark: Great!

B. Ask your partner.

How old were you last year?
How old will you be next year?
What did you do last summer?
What will you do next summer?

C. Answer the question.

What's in your refrigerator at home?

D. Listen and circle.

a few apples   a lot of apples

a little potato salad   a lot of potato salad

a little ham   a lot of ham

a few cookies   a lot of cookies

a little milk   a lot of milk

a few eggs   a lot of eggs

E. Play a game. Ask and answer.

A: How many peaches are there?
B: There are | a few | peaches.
           | a lot of |

A: How much cake is there?
B: There is | a little | cake.
          | a lot of |

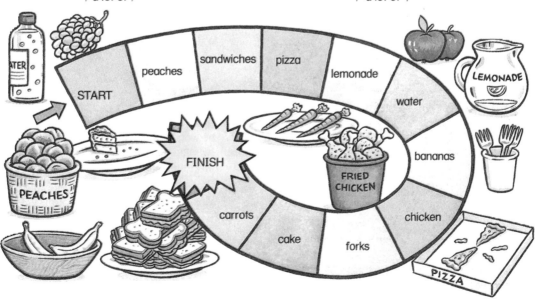

Anna: Who's that?
Kevin: That's me when I was two years old.
Anna: That's a cute picture.

Anna: What about that picture? Is that you, too?
Kevin: Yeah.
Anna: When did you learn how to ride a bike?
Kevin: Oh, I don't remember. I think I was four years old.
Anna: Did you want to be a firefighter?
Kevin: Yes, I did. And that bike was my fire engine.

Kevin: What about you? What did you want to be when you were little?
Anna: I wanted to be a police officer, and a ballerina, and a princess!

What did you want to be when you were little?
I wanted to be a police officer.

Ask and answer.

When did he learn how to ride a bike?
He learned how to ride a bike when he was six.

1. ride a bike
six

2. play baseball
seven

3. do a somersault
four

4. do a cartwheel
nine

5. do a handstand
eight

6. write his name
four

7. swim
six

8. read
five

What about you?

When did you learn how to ride a bike?

Let's Learn

When the bell rang this morning, the students went into the classroom. It was 8:30, but the teacher wasn't there.

At 8:45, the teacher walked into the classroom. It was very noisy. Some students were working, but other students were talking and laughing.

When the students saw the teacher, they ran back to their seats. Suddenly the classroom was quiet.

Then the teacher heard a funny noise. He looked around the room. Oh, no! Mark was snoring!

Grammar Focus	
The students were working **when the teacher walked into the room.**	**When the teacher walked into the room,** the students were working.

Ask and answer.

What was she doing when the doorbell rang?
She **was** doing her homework when the doorbell rang.

What were you doing when the teacher walked into the classroom today?

OR

What was your teacher doing when you walked into the classroom today?

Alice's Report

Last year I went on a homestay to the United States. I lived with the Johnson family in the state of California. When I was there, I went to school with my American sister, Julie.

At first, speaking English every day was hard. I was homesick. But then I started to enjoy my homestay. English was easier. School was fun. I liked living with the Johnsons.

During spring vacation, I went camping with my host family. We slept in a tent and went hiking in the woods.

Now I'm back home. I often write to my American family and they write to me. Next year the Johnsons are going to visit me.

New Words

homestay	homesick
state	enjoy
California	host family
American	slept

Answer the questions.

1. What did Alice do last year?
2. In her American family, did Alice have any brothers or sisters?
3. What did the Johnsons do during spring vacation?
4. When will Alice see the Johnson family again?

True or false?

1. Alice went on a homestay to Canada.
2. At first, speaking English was easy for Alice.
3. Alice didn't like living with the Johnsons.
4. The Johnsons often write to Alice.

Choose a title.

Which is the best title for Alice's report?
a. Alice's Homestay
b. The Johnson Family
c. Camping in the United States

Vocabulary

What does "homestay" mean?
a. stay at home with your own family
b. stay in another country with your own family
c. stay in another country with another family

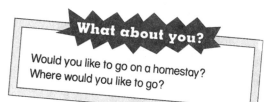

What about you?

Would you like to go on a homestay?
Where would you like to go?

Sounds and Sentences

photo

photographer

phantom

phone

The photographer took a photo of the phantom on the phone.

knight

knock

knuckles

knees

The knight knocked his knuckles on his knees.

How Old Were You?

How old were you when you learned how to run?
    I was one.
    I was one.
How old were you when you went to the zoo?
    I was two.
    I was two.
How old were you when you started to ski?
    I was three.
    I was three.
How old were you when you helped at the store?
    I was four.
    I was four.
How old were you when you learned how to dive?
    I was five.
    I was five.

I was five when I learned how to dive.
I was four when I helped at the store.
I was three when I started to ski.
I was two when I went to the zoo.
I was one when I learned how to run.

True or false? Listen and circle the answer.

| 1. true | 2. true | 3. true | 4. true | 5. true | 6. true |
| false | false | false | false | false | false |

Listen and write the letter.

____ 1. Bill learned how to do a somersault
____ 2. Jenny learned how to ride a bike
____ 3. When Robin was eight
____ 4. When Andy was nine
____ 5. Barb learned how to do a cartwheel
____ 6. When Dale was five

a. when she was six.
b. when she was seven.
c. he learned how to play baseball.
d. he learned how to write his name.
e. she learned how to do a handstand.
f. when he was four.

Beth: Anna, look!
Anna: What is it?
Beth: It's an airplane ticket. I'm going to France this summer! I'm going to visit my relatives.
Anna: Wow! When are you going?
Beth: In July. I'll be there for three weeks.

Anna: Have you ever been to France?
Beth: No, I haven't. I've never been out of the country.
Anna: Me neither. Who are you going with?
Beth: That's the exciting part! I'm going with my cousin Jane. I've never traveled without my parents before.

Anna: Oh Beth, you're so lucky!
Beth: Yes, but there's only one problem.
Anna: What?
Beth: I don't speak French.

I've never been out of the country.
  Me neither.

I have = I've

Ask and answer.

Have you ever | eaten burritos?
| seen a penguin?

  Yes, I have.
  No, I haven't.

eat → eaten
see → seen
be → been

1. burritos

2. sushi

3. potato salad

4. fried rice

5. a penguin

6. a kangaroo

7. a llama

8. a cheetah

Make sentences.

I've been to _____ , but I've never been to _____ .
I've eaten _____ , but I've never eaten _____ .
I've seen _____ , but I've never seen _____ .

Beth is on her way to France. She has been on an airplane before, but she has never been out of the country. She can't wait. She has never seen the Eiffel Tower and she has never used French money. She has never spoken to a French person and she has never eaten French food. Beth is going to try all these things for the first time.

Grammar Focus

bake	→ have baked	go	→ have gone	speak	→ have spoken
be	→ have been	read	→ have read	stay up	→ have stayed up
drive	→ have driven	ride	→ have ridden	use	→ have used
eat	→ have eaten	see	→ have seen	watch	→ have watched
fly	→ have flown	sleep	→ have slept	write	→ have written

Play a game. Ask and answer.

Have you ever baked cookies?
   Yes, I have.
   No, I haven't.

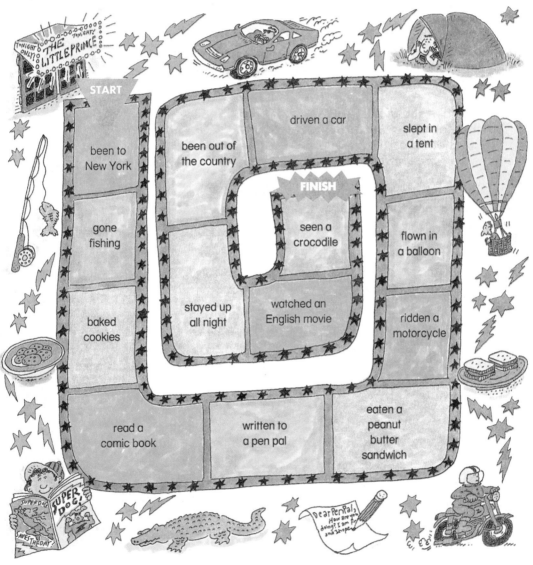

START

been to
New York

been out of
the country

driven a car

slept in
a tent

gone
fishing

FINISH

seen a
crocodile

flown in
a balloon

baked
cookies

stayed up
all night

watched an
English movie

ridden a
motorcycle

read a
comic book

written to
a pen pal

eaten a
peanut
butter
sandwich

Beth's Report

Have you ever been to Paris? I was there this summer. It is a fun place to visit! Here are some things to do in Paris.

Eat breakfast outside at a sidewalk cafe. I liked the hot chocolate and pastries.

Take a walk along the Seine River. You can see many artists painting and selling their pictures. You can buy books and postcards, too.

Ride the Metro to the Eiffel Tower. The view from the top is great day and night.

Visit the park near the Eiffel Tower. There is a puppet theater in the park. You can see a very funny puppet show there.

Just remember one thing. Learn some French words before you go. Then you can speak French in Paris!

New Words

Paris
place
sidewalk cafe
hot chocolate
pastries
along
Seine River

Metro
Eiffel Tower
view
puppet theater
funny
puppet show

Answer the questions

1. Where can you eat breakfast in Paris?
2. What can you buy along the Seine River?
3. Where is there a puppet theater in Paris?
4. Can you go to the top of the Eiffel Tower at night?

True or false?

1. You can eat pastries and drink hot chocolate at cafes.
2. The Metro goes to the Eiffel Tower.
3. There is a puppet show on the Eiffel Tower.
4. People in France speak French.

Choose a title.

Which is the best title for Beth's report?
a. Puppet Shows
b. Visiting Paris
c. The Eiffel Tower

Vocabulary

What does "sidewalk cafe" mean?
a. a restaurant with tables inside
b. a restaurant with tables outside
c. a restaurant inside a store

What about you?

Have you ever been to Paris?
Which big cities have you visited?

Sounds and Sentences

what
whale
whiskers
whisper
white

What did the whale with whiskers whisper to the white whale?

wren
wrap
wrench
wreath

Have you ever seen a wren wrap a wrench and a wreath?

Have You Ever Broken Your Elbow?

Have you ever broken your elbow?
Have you ever eaten a snail?
Have you ever ridden a rhino?
Or stepped on a lion's tail?

No, I've never broken my elbow.
I've never eaten a snail.
I've never ridden a rhino.
Or stepped on a lion's tail.

Have you ever driven a taxi?
Have you ever flown your own plane?
Have you ever forgotten your book bag?
On a bus in the middle of Spain?

No, I've never driven a taxi.
I've never flown my own plane.
But one day I forgot my beautiful book bag
On a bus in the middle of Spain.

Listen and check.

✔ = yes   ✘ = no

Kelly	✔	✔	✘	✔	✔	✘
Drew	✘	✘	✔	✘	✔	✔

1. Yes, he has.   2. Yes, she has.   3. Yes, he has.   4. Yes, she has.
    No, he hasn't.   No, she hasn't.   No, he hasn't.   No, she hasn't.

Listen and fill in the chart.

✔ = yes   ✘ = no

	slept in a tent	seen a crocodile	gone fishing	been to New York	flown in a balloon	ridden a motorcycle
Rob						
Lori						
Adam						
Kristy						
Debbie						
Paul						

Unit 8   73

A. Fill in the blanks. Then say and act.

1. **Anna:** Did you want _____
   when you were little?
   Kevin: Yes, _____. And that bike was my
   fire engine. What about you? _____
   _____ when you were
   little?
   Anna: I _____.

2. **Anna:** Have you ever _____ France?
   Beth: No, _____. I've never been out of
   the country.
   Anna: Me neither. Who _____?
   Beth: That's the exciting part! I'm going with

   _____.

B. Ask your partner.

When did you learn how to ride a bike?
When did you learn how to do a somersault?
When did you learn how to write your name?
When did you learn how to read?

C. Answer the question.

Have you ever been out of the country?
Where did you go?

D. Listen and number the pictures.

What were the children doing when it started to rain?

E. Ask your friends.

Have you ever _____?

Names	me				
ridden a horse					
flown in an airplane					
gone camping					
seen a kangaroo					
been to Australia					
eaten potato salad					

UNIT	Language Items	Functions	Topics
1	I'm (Beth). I'm (12). I'm (10) years old. My name's (Mark). My best friend is (Anna). What's (her) name? (Her) name is (Beth). How old is (she)? (She's) (10) years old. Does (she) have any brothers or sisters? (She) has (two brothers). (She) doesn't have any (brothers or sisters). What does (she) like to do? (She) likes to (play computer games). What did (she) do during vacation? (She) went (to math camp) during vacation. What does (she) want to be? (She) wants to be (an engineer). What is (he) going to do? (He's) going to (play soccer). What does (he) have to do? (He) has to (wash the dishes). What did (they) do yesterday? (They) went to (the zoo). What does (he) want to do? (He) wants to (sail a boat). Why did (she) stay home yesterday? (She) stayed home because (she had a stomachache). Which one is (bigger)? The (dog) is (bigger).	Self-identification Asking about and expressing one's age Describing who people are Asking about and describing what someone did during vacation Asking about and describing what someone wants to be Asking about and describing what someone likes to do	Introductions Family Comparisons Activities Occupations
2	Have a good trip. Thanks. See you Monday. What does (he) look like? (He) has (red hair) and (green eyes). Which (girl) is (Brian's cousin)? (His cousin) is the (girl) with (curly red hair). /(Her aunt) is the (woman) in the (yellow cap).	Wishing someone a good time Describing people's hair color and style Describing people's eye color Identifying people by their clothing and features	Family Physical appearance
3	Would you like to (go camping) with us? Sure! I'd love to. Thanks, but I can't. (He's) going to (go camping). What will (he) need? (He'll) need (a tent) and (a flashlight). What will (they) do tomorrow? (They'll) go canoeing. It'll be (hot) tomorrow. I'll need (a jacket). I won't need (a jacket).	Extending, accepting, and declining invitations Talking about the future using "will" Asking about and expressing needs Describing tomorrow's temperature	Outdoor activities and equipment Temperature

UNIT	Language Items	Functions	Topics

4	What do you think?
	  I think (geography) is (easy).
	I think (geography) is (easier) than
	  (science).
	Which subject is (easier), (geography) or
	  (science)?
	Which one is the (fastest)?
	  The (cheetah) is the (fastest).
	The (fox) is as (fast) as the (kangaroo).
		Eliciting and expressing
		  personal opinion
		Comparing school subjects
		Comparing animal sizes and
		  speeds
			School subjects
			Animals

5	Wait for (us). OK.
	Why does (he) like (winter) best?
	  (He) likes (winter) best because (he)
	  likes (ice skating).
	What did (she) do (last summer)?
	  (She) went (to a dude ranch).
	What is (she) going to do (next summer)?
	  (She's) going to go (to the beach).
		Requesting that someone wait
		Asking about and expressing
		  personal preference
		Asking about and stating what
		  someone did
		Asking about and stating what
		  someone is going to do
			Seasons
			Seasonal
			  activities

6	Why don't we (make a snack)?
	  That's a good idea. No, I don't want to.
	There is some (juice).
	There are some (cookies).
	How much (water) is there?
	  There is a little (water).
	  There is a lot of (water).
	How many (oranges) are there?
	  There are a few (oranges).
	  There are a lot of (oranges).
		Making, agreeing with, and
		  declining suggestions
		Asking about and stating
		  quantities
			Countable and
			  non countable
			  food items

7	What did you want to be when you were
	  little? I wanted to be (a ballerina).
	When did (he) learn how to (ride a bike)?
	  (He) learned how to (ride a bike) when
	  (he) was (six).
	What was (she) doing when (the doorbell
	  rang)? (She) was (doing her homework)
	  when (the doorbell rang).
	When (the doorbell rang) (she) was
	  (doing her homework).
		Talking about childhood hopes
		  and dreams
		Asking and stating when
		  someone learned to do
		  something
		Asking and stating what
		  someone was doing when
		  something else happened
			Childhood hopes
			  and dreams
			Childhood
			  milestones

8	Have you ever (been to France)?
	  Yes, I have.
	  No, I haven't.
	I've (seen a penguin) but I've never (seen
	  a cheetah).
		Asking and talking about
		  experiences
			New and prior
			  experiences
			Travel

Word List

A

a 4
about 9
afraid 34
after 20
afternoon 24
again 32
ago 34
airplane 66
all 8
along 70
also 4
always 9
am 12
American 62
an 6
and 4
animals 6
another 63
answer 28
answered 44
any 4
anything 46
anywhere 12
apartment 16
apples 51
are 5
around 27
art 31
artists 70
as 33
ask 22
at 4
ate 34
aunt 12
Australia 44
away 16

B

back 42
backpack 25
bait 25
bake 68
baked 68
ballerina 58
balloon 69
bananas 48
barns 8
baseball 23
baseball bat 18
basket 49
bathing suit 23
be 6
beach 43
beautiful 26
because 34
been 66
before 66

behind 8
bell 60
bench 12
best 4
better 36
big 16
bigger 7
biggest 33
bike 58
bike riding 39
binoculars 25
bird 4
bird watching 25
birthday cards 26
black 13
blond 13
blue 13
board 31
bones 34
book bag 72
books 32
both 30
bottom 52
bought 46
boy 9
Brachiosaurus 34
bread 48
breakfast 70
bright 18
bring 22
broken 72
brothers 4
brown 13
build 6
built 6
burritos 67
bus 8
but 8
buy 46

C

cafe 70
cages 8
cake 49
California 62
camp 5
campfire 24
campground 24
camping 7
can 8
can't 8
Canada 63
canoe 25
canoeing 24
cap 14
car 22
carefully 26
carrots 49
cartwheel 59
cat 33

catch 40
chart 32
cheese 48
cheetah 33
chicken 34
Chile 16
chocolate 50
choose 52
cities 71
class 32
classroom 60
clean up 7
clothes 22
coach 6
coins 31
cold 23
coldest 44
collecting 27
come 28
comic book 69
coming 14
compared 32
Compsognathus 34
computer games 4
computers 6
cookies 49
count 49
country 45
cousins 12
crocodile 36
cry 36
cupboard 48
cups 49
curly 13
cute 58

D

dark 36
day 6
December 44
decided 50
delicious 50
desserts 50
did 5
didn't 63
different 8
dinner 42
dinosaur 34
disappointed 50
dishes 7
dive 64
do 5
does 5
doesn't 5
dogs 4
doing 21
don't 4
door 16
doorbell 61
down 17

draw 6
dress 14
drink 71
drive 68
driven 68
dry 26
dude ranch 42
during 4

E

each 16
easier 30
easy 30
eat 35
eaten 67
eggs 52
Eiffel Tower 68
eight 59
elbow 72
elephant 36
else 27
engineer 6
England 16
English 31
English teacher 10
enjoy 62
even 36
ever 9
every 6
everyone 42
everything 50
exciting 66
eyes 13

F

fall 41
family 16
far 16
fast 32
faster 32
fastest 32
fat 52
father 10
favorite 31
feathers 34
February 45
feeds 6
fences 8
few 50
fierce 34
fight 34
find 26
fire engine 58
firefighter 58
first 22

first prize 6
fish 4
fishing 24
fishing pole 25
five 12
flashlight 23
flea 36
flew 34
flowers 41
flown 68
fly 35,36,41
food 50
football 41
for 6
forgot 72
forgotten 72
forks 49
four 58
fox 33
France 66
free 8
French 66
fried rice 67
friend 4
from 53
fruits 52
full 50
fun 22
funny 60
future 42

G

games 6
gazelle 33
gentle 8
geography 31
get 26
girl 14
gives 6
glasses 12
glue 26
go 7
goal 6
goes 71
going 7
gone 68
good 6
grade 43
grains 52
grandfather 15
grandmother 15
grandparents 5
gray 13
great 22
green 13
greyhound 33
groups 53
grow 52

H

had 32
hair 13
ham 48
handstand 59
happy 53
hard 30
harder 30
has 7
hasn't 73
hate 40
have 4
haven't 66
Hawaii 46
he 6
he'll 23
he's 7
healthy 52
heard 60
hello 22
help 32
helped 64
helper 4
her 5
here 12
hey 30
hi 4
hiking 24
hiking boots 25
his 5
history 31
home 7,8
homesick 62
homestay 62
homework 61
horse 42
host 62
hot 23
hot chocolate 70
hour 26
house 16
how 5
hungry 48
hurry 40

I

I 4
I'd 22
I'll 23
I'm 4
I've 72
ice 44
ice cream 49
ice skating 41
idea 48
important 52
in 8
inside 8

straight 13
strawberries 35
stream 35
striped 14
stroller 35
stronger 36
students 60
subject 31
suddenly 60
sugar 52
summer 41
sun 28
Sunday 24
sunny 44
sure 22
surprised 32
sushi 67
swallows 17
swan 17
sweater 36
swim 59
swimming 23
swing 17
swooped 17

T

tables 71
tail 72
talking 60
tall 12
taller 34
taxi 72
tea 46
teacher 21
teddy bear 18
teeth 34
tennis 23
tennis ball 23
tennis racquet 23
tent 23
test 30
than 30
thanks 12
that 12
that's 18
the 4
their 9
them 6
then 24
there 12
there's 40
thermos 25
these 8
they 7
they'll 23
they're 7
things 26
think 30
thinking 15
this 16

those 54
thought 44
three 64
through 8
ticket 66
tie 46
time 42
times 44
tired 40
title 9
to 4
today 34
told 42
tomorrow 20
tonight 28
too 10
too much 26
took 32
top 52
toss 31
touch 8
towel 23
train 8
traveled 66
trip 24
try 52
Tuesday 45
twenty 22
twilight 17
twinkling 17
twins 17
twirled 17
two 4
two-dollar 46
Tyrannosaurus
    Rex 34

U

uncle 14
United States 44
up 40
us 22
use 26
used 68
usually 8

V

vacation 4
vegetables 52
very 6
veterinarian 6
view 70
visited 5
visiting 71
volleyball 7

W

wait 26
waiting 12
walk 70
walked 34
walking 40
wanted 58
wants 6
warm 23
was 4
wash 7
wasn't 60
watch 8
watched 68
water 6
water skiing 41
way 24
we're 40
wears 12
weather 28
weatherman 28
Wednesday 45
week 42
weekend 22
well 12
went 4
were 34
whale 71
what 5
what's 5
when 44
where 9
which 7
whiskers 71
white 71
who 66
who's 5
why 7
wife 10
wild 8
wild animal park 8
will 22
winter 41
with 4
without 66
woman 14
won 6
won't 23
woods 62
words 70
worked 42
working 60
world 44
worried 30
would 22
wow 66
wrap 71
wrapping paper 26
wreath 71
wren 71
wrench 71

write 59
written 68

Y

yeah 58
year 16
years 4
yellow 14
yes 12
yesterday 7
you 5
you'll 23
you're 66
younger 15
your 5

Z

zoo 4